Imaginary Superstar
Surviving and Thriving
Through Workforce Warfare

DR. WANDA J CORNER PH.D.

Imaginary Superstar
Published by
Corner of Success, Inc.
Atlanta, GA

Corner of Success, Inc.
ISBN-13: 978-0692212059
ISBN-10: 0692212051
Library of Congress Control Number: 2014939976
Corner of Success, Inc, Atlanta, GA

Printed in the United States of America
www.imaginarysuperstar.com

Dedication

This book is dedicated to my biggest fan,
my husband, James.
You have supported every life dream
I have had since we have been married.

Acknowledgments

I WOULD LIKE TO ACKNOWLEDGE my mother for helping me develop work ethic, integrity, and self-confidence in accomplishing every life dream with hard work. Most importantly, I thank her for allowing me to always share and help others. And Of course, for being the "Kool-Aid" mom when I was growing up, even though I didn't realize we did not have a lot to give.

I would also like to acknowledge my friends and colleagues who encouraged me to write this book, based on their own experiences. A special thanks to the Power Ladies, two of whom have gone before me to write their inspirational books.

Table of Contents

Foreword

THIS BOOK IS ABOUT PERSONAL healing and hope in the midst of workplace warfare. The reality of today's contemporary workplace includes diversity, innovation, technology, and human capital cobbled together in a rapid cycle of moving parts. Without the ability to self-reflect, it is difficult to navigate our way through the people aspect of workforce adversity (human evil, deceit, jealousy, and unethical behavior). We must first identify and commit to our true authentic selves. Otherwise, we can become casualties of workforce warfare by succumbing to those undesirable and deviant behaviors that we consider unacceptable. This first installment of the *Imaginary Superstar* series will focus on assisting you in identifying your True Authentic Self (TAS), while committing to the attainment of performance excellence and personal peace through positive behavior and communication.

Introduction

WHEN I FIRST CAME UP with the title for this book, *Imaginary Superstar*, I thought it was going to be focused on leaders who exuded the confidence level that is earned by genuine, hard-working, technically, emotionally, and professionally competent individuals. Sadly, I discovered that these leaders did not possess one of those traits/characteristics. Rather, they had been given the gift of leadership without the hard work of earning it. This may have been due to a merit-based promotion, nepotism, or a number of other unearned accomplishments. In any event, these individuals' organizations suffered under the weight of poor leadership. Irrespective of how they obtained the leadership title, they had both the privilege and responsibility to professionally develop themselves, as well as those they oversee.

Now, after eight years of keeping my observation notes in an electronic folder, I finally decided to start writing this book. My biggest challenge was trying to decide which topics to discuss. Rather than trying to fit it all in one book, I decided to approach this book project as an anthology (series under a brand name with varying types of documents and media). In this light, this first installment focuses on building a deliberate foundation to overcome a toxic work environment in which evil and negativity can lead to an erosion of human decency and business ethics.

During a negative past experience on the job, I remember one of my colleagues saying to me, "You should watch your back." She was referring to the fact that I was exceeding the performance expectations and thereby threatening the status quo. My response to her was, "If I am always watching my back, I may miss the opportunities and blessings right in front of me." I just refused to get distracted by a false paranoia based on a potentially imaginary jealousy, deceit, and other people's fear.

CHAPTER 1
What Is the Meaning of "Imaginary Superstar" (IS)?

JEALOUSY, DECEIT, AND FEAR SHOULD have no longevity in the minds of those who aspire to uncompromised performance excellence (both personally and professionally). That's it! On that note, this first installment of the series is about imagining and becoming a superstar performer in your career over a period of time, without succumbing to the potential pitfalls of negativity and human evil in the workplace. Let's face it: you spend an inordinate amount of time in your career; probably more than anywhere else you choose or have to be.

CONCEPT OF TIME IN YOUR CAREER
Let's discuss the concept of time during your professional career. Suppose you started your career clock ticking after graduating from college at an average age of twenty-two to twenty-five years old. How much time would you spend on the job in a forty-hour week up to the age of sixty-five (including vacation and sick days)?

ESTIMATED CAREER TIMETABLE

College Graduation Age	40 Hours per Week	52 Weeks per Year	Estimated Hours/ Year	Times Retirement at 65 Years	Total Career Hours Worked
22	40	52	2080	43 years	89,440
23	40	52	2080	42 years	87,360
24	40	52	2080	41 years	85,280
25	40	52	2080	40 years	83,200

As you can see in the Estimated Career Timetable above, we spend a great deal of our lives in the workplace. During this period of time, there is an assumption that we are conscious and alert. Most importantly, we are communicating and engaging in human behavior, with some exceptions. There is a great deal of time and opportunity to view and treat our careers as a positive extension of who we are, or who we choose to be. It is left up to us to decide how much of who we really are that we want to expose. Furthermore, we can choose to utilize the same hours shown in the Career Timetable to expose others to the very best in us or the very worst in us. We are accountable for our own success.

In order to develop a sustainable level of professional excellence and personal peace, we must first determine what we will be willing to do in order to attain this individual goal. What sacrifices (if any) will you be willing or able to make? In some instances, it may entail you leaving or staying in your current position. If you have to stay, are you willing to do the work necessary for attaining or developing personal peace? Alternatively, if you have to leave, are you financially in a position to do so? These are some of the tough questions that we may have to ask ourselves to alleviate work-related stress caused by workforce warfare.

I prefer to focus on that which can be controlled, which is my own self. The same holds true for you, as a professional. Although you cannot change others, you can teach them how you want to be treated, as well as how they can expect for you to treat them. If others fall short, you have the option to forgive them, ignore them, correct them, and/ or choose to develop extraordinary communication skills that result in personal peace. In fact, you may have to use any or even all of these behavioral and communication techniques to secure mutual respect and dignity with your respective role(s) as a manager, peer, coworker, customer, client, board member, etc.

The personal peace to which I am referring is facilitated by intervention techniques to maintain performance excellence during the entire life cycle of your career. However, the techniques work best if you are dealing with rational human beings, which is not always within your control.

In subsequent sections of this book, you will read examples of how to deal with irrational people while maintaining a professional decorum (through candid communication). In some of these examples, professional instincts and career survival may take precedence for the purposes of emotional and personal safety.

CHAPTER 2
Leadership Performance Excellence

THE MORE YOU WORK ON yourself as an individual, the better prepared you will be in overcoming any challenges that you may encounter in the workforce. If you want to leave your options open for becoming a future leader, it is critical that you develop the emotional, technical, and self-reflection skills you need to best facilitate success through others. Be honest about your strengths, weaknesses, and experiences that may affect your ability to move, inspire, and motivate others.

Earlier, I discussed the potentially catastrophic outcomes of unearned/poor leadership such as: high turnover of critical skilled/key employees, allegations of malfeasance, employer related lawsuits, negative publicity, and major loss of income/revenues. Unearned leadership titles are no excuse for incompetence. True leaders should recognize whether they have the potential for developing proficiency in critical skills relevant to their positions. Otherwise, they should step aside, step down, or "step out" of the organization. This simply means that they are not a fit for the organizational leadership needs. It takes a very strong person to admit to that to him- or herself, let alone to an organization.

As a realist, I know that it is highly unlikely that leaders will admit they are incompetent. However, they can "save face" by finding positions in which they do not have to be in constant fear when their incompetence is either discovered or glaringly apparent.

IS—MOVING TOWARD SUPERSTAR OPTIONS

Becoming a superstar in your professional career usually starts with obtaining employment. Whether you are self-employed or an employee of a business enterprise, it is important that you make a series of correct decisions. The decisions you make now may determine the number of options you have later. Unfortunately, there is no guarantee that the career-focused decisions you make will be validated now or later. In any event, you need to start with self.

It is the True Authentic Self (TAS) that will either draw others to you or repel them from you. What do I mean by the authentic self? Although there are several written references to the authentic self and its definition, I am defining the True Authentic Self as the core of who you are, including your values and your expectations of self and others.

CHAPTER 3
Discovering My True Authentic Self

DURING MY UNDERGRADUATE DEGREE, I changed my major from political science to communications. After all, I had been speaking publicly for years. It was a space that brought me a challenging sense of comfort and accomplishment over the years. I have always been intrigued by the power of the spoken and written word, whether I was taking part in the "Gettysburg Address" competition in elementary school or giving the class speech for my high school graduation. Public speaking may be utilized for good or evil. I believe that those of us who learn how to facilitate its power for positive social and behavioral change can make a difference in any environment.

Over the years, I have been asked to speak to various groups about the subject of entrepreneurship. Nothing feels better to me than to have an opportunity to inspire others to "win" in their quest for success. Aside from earning my PhD, my role as an entrepreneur (for the last 14 years) has been the loneliest, challenging, and fulfilling accomplishment of my life. It requires focus, commitment, and adaptive leadership, even in the wake of uncertainty. Now, I enter this new chapter of my life, writing my first book, without the complexity of scholarly writing and research. So far, the experience is challenging, liberating, and scary all at once. Nevertheless, the next fifty-plus pages exemplify the *risk-taking* characteristic that every true entrepreneur possesses.

FOR GOOD OR EVIL

Effective communication skills may be used for good or evil. When I graduated from undergraduate school, I was not prepared for my future workforce experience. To compound the complexity of finding a professional job, I had not utilized the career services department or tried to get an internship. As a person who worked to pay my own way through college, I simply had not planned for life after graduation. This is contradictory to my personality traits. However, I was so fatigued from working (sixty-plus hours per week) to pay for tuition and living expenses, I failed to plan for this critical phase of my life. In an effort to catch up, I decided to attend every college business job fair that the university sponsored.

I planned which companies I wanted to speak to about potential opportunities when I arrived at the job fair. In 1989, the Internet was not yet a source for instant access to business resources. As a result, I had an opportunity to see if my degree in communications was going to pay off.

With resume in hand and a professional demeanor, I was armed with confidence. After all, either I was prepared or not. I approached the companies that piqued my interest, having read their materials before arriving at their exhibit tables. Then, the game was on. I began to sell my skills to the recruiters based on my background and interest, relevant to the position. Although I did not have the specific educational degree that they were looking for, apparently my communication skills showed promise.

Prior to securing my first management position (as a college graduate), I went through a series of interviews at the top levels of the company all within one day. I was so fatigued at "being drilled" relevant to my interest and skill that I had no energy for anything short of sincere and honest responses. Furthermore, I had to drive forty-five minutes each way for the interview process. At the end of the ordeal, I thought that I probably did not get the job because of my candor.

I remember taking a nap when I returned home from the interview marathon and then going to visit a friend to take my mind off my impending defeat. Within a couple of hours, however, I received a call offering me the position. I thought to myself, perhaps staying true to who I am is the best approach for career success. I have continued this same approach, although it has not always been easy, throughout my career and consulting practice.

At fifty years of age, I believe that I have garnered enough first-hand, as well as vicarious learning experiences about leadership and the workforce to share with others. My hope is that this book will help others reflect and think deeply about how their communication skills may increase their capacity to progress in their professional career. Most importantly, I hope this book will encourage leaders and employees to utilize positive behavioral and communication skills to overcome the challenges of human evil in the workplace.

WHAT MAKES A LEADER?

I am very direct about the topic of leadership. Sadly, some people believe that they are leaders because they have followers. The importance of having earned a position of leadership seems to have evaded them. Leadership is both a privilege and a gift of responsibility. In some cases, it may make you a better person or a worse one. In either case, along with leadership comes an inherent responsibility to not only care about the welfare of the organization but about the people who do the work.

Now that the business world is becoming more focused on human talent, the interdependence of an organization's sustainability will be focused on the top leadership's ability to leverage human capital within its workforce. Concurrently, the cadre of leadership throughout the hierarchy of the organization (if any) requires basic technical, emotional, communication, and organizational management competence.

Let me first operationalize the words *competent* and *incompetent*, as some people gasp when I describe someone as being incompetent. If *competent* means possessing the knowledge, skills, and ability for effective action, then *incompetent* means lacking the knowledge, skills, and abilities for effective action. This is an important word in today's competitive marketplace.

Relevant to leadership performance, *incompetence* is a word that people seem unwilling to use. In many cases, they even feel that it is an insult. The word should not be viewed as an insult but rather a way of expressing some organizational performance challenge that needs to be addressed. Sometimes it is possible to address the challenge with professional development. In other cases, there simply is not an "organizational fit" between the employee/leader and the current organization.

Identifying talent gaps (especially in leadership) and addressing professional development needs within the organization are critical skills focused on human talent, which should be in alignment with the needs of the organization.

MANAGING EMPLOYEE PERFORMANCE CHALLENGES

Because human capital is a major competitive asset, retaining an employee who lacks the prerequisite skills can be a liability. As a leader, it is your responsibility to determine whether incompetent employees can't or won't perform according to the needs of the job/position. In either scenario, your first management approach for performance-based issues should be that you are there to assist employees in their professional success. In this light, ask them what their personal self-assessment is of their performance. What do they see as their strengths and weaknesses relevant to the job description and expectations?

Let's first take a step back and clarify that the employees have verifiable performance expectations:

- Were they provided with an updated job description within the last year?
- Did they provide a confirmation of their job description update within the last year?
- Have they been evaluated at least annually?

An annual performance review is not a time to reveal surprise expectations. A leader should ensure that employees know what their performance expectations are, based on verifiable documentation. Without this minimum criteria, there is the prospect for missed opportunities for teaching, personal accountability, and professional growth.

Although performance evaluations are a benchmark, they are not the "end all, be all" for performance. A manager should utilize the performance evaluation as a baseline for mutual dialogue with the employee. This should be a transition point for the next step, which is the personal self-assessment.

EMPLOYEE PERSONAL SELF-ASSESSMENT

By utilizing the personal self-assessment, you will more than likely gain a nonconfrontational opportunity to discover your employee's construct of reality (individual perception of self and the environment), as it relates to his or her performance. Also, it will provide an opportunity for you to start with a baseline for the development of a corrective action plan, if needed.

If the employee's personal self-assessment is incongruent with yours, aside from developing a corrective action plan, you should determine whether the individual can't or won't do the job for which he or she has been hired.

A number of years ago, I was a supervisor, experiencing my first performance evaluation with my manager. I knew that I exceeded the performance expectations and had expressed that on my performance self-assessment. During my annual evaluation, my manager actually told me that my performance was superior and exceeded expectations, but that she would not give anyone a superior performance rating in their evaluation. This was completely irrational. When I asked her what criteria she was using and how I could attain the "superior performance level," she became indignant, rather than taking the opportunity as a teaching moment. I could only surmise that she had no reason for giving me less than a superior performance. My point is that performance evaluations should force the employee to reach, yet a high performance level should be attainable. Otherwise, the self-assessment will be perceived as a disingenuous method of approaching employee development. In my case, I clearly fell into the category of - "She can do the job", but my own self-assessment was incongruent with my supervisor. Rather than mentoring me (as I was a supervisor myself), she felt threatened.

Alternatively, if employees do not have the necessary skills for acceptable performance, they fall into the category of "They can't do the job." In this instance, the leader should try multiple methods to increase their proficiency in the needed areas of weakness. For example, you might try one or all of the following:

- Peer-to-peer mentoring
- Formal professional development training (webinars, professional coach, in-class training, workshops, etc.)
- Scheduled one-on-one training with them directly

If these methods do not work, you may want to consult with the human resources management team for advice on other resources that you may not have utilized to assist the employee.

If employees do not have what I call a "willful intent" to succeed, then they fall into the category of "They won't do the job." In this instance, a manager must lead them toward personal accountability for their success or failure. This may be done using the following approach:

- Review the performance evaluation and discuss how they may best improve. This should include specific examples of measurement over a ninety-day corrective action plan that is reviewed and clearly documented.
- Ask them whether they are willing to work toward the performance goals to meet the performance expectations and timelines.
- If they express their willingness, have them commit to the agreement by signing and dating the corrective action plan.
- Communicate the expectations that you will follow up with a progress review in alignment with the documented corrective action plan every thirty days to enable mutual understanding of their status.

At the end of ninety days, the final review should not only include review of their ninety-day performance, but include a current status of employment, as well as future performance expectations.

The purpose in following this ninety-day corrective plan is two-fold. First, it gives employees an opportunity to discuss and clarify expectations each month. Second, it gives employees an opportunity to preserve their dignity and seek other employment if they can't or won't do the job for which they have been hired.

As a manager in public, nonprofit, and private sectors, I have followed the ninety-day corrective action plan outlined above, not only for the organization's sake, but for the employee's sake, as well. Following these plans also allows me to achieve my goal of staying true to my authentic self, which includes compassion for others.

In the instances where I have had to terminate employees (whether they can't or won't do the job), a few of them have actually thanked me later. I certainly did not expect that to happen. By establishing co-accountability for performance expectations, I was able to meet my responsibilities in facilitating their success or helping them to recognize the lack of organizational fit, at minimum.

I am always saddened when I hear that employees were unexpectedly fired or laid off. I think it is cowardly for a manager to fire someone with little to no notification, except in circumstances in which it could not be helped (sudden loss of revenue, extreme environmental factors such as natural disaster, corporate downsizing, or merger/acquisition).

Even though I worked and paid my way through college, I was unaware that the biggest challenge I would face would be knowing how to deal with what I call "workplace warfare." According to *Merriam-Webster*'s definition of warfare, the word means "activity that is done as part of a struggle between competing groups, companies, etc." If I apply this same concept to my professional experience as a manager, leader, employee, and consultant, it has been a constant struggle between my True Authentic Self and my work environment.

My True Authentic Self includes my moral, ethical, and spiritual beliefs about how I should treat others, as well as my expectations of how others treat me. Overall, everyone should be treated with dignity, respect, equity, and fairness.

In my youth and naiveté, I actually thought earning a college degree would, in and of itself, escalate me to an environment that reflected mutual integrity and fairness. However, what I found was this toxic environment (during most of my career) that I had to learn to navigate on my own terms. Of course, this knowledge came with a price, which I decided to pay in exchange for personal peace. The outcome was my ability to observe the work environment, as both a participant and an observer.

Being both a participant and an observer enabled me to reflect on some of the best and worst times of my professional and consulting career. As a lifelong learner, I am willing to share some of those experiences to help others to reflect and navigate through workplace warfare without becoming casualties of a toxic work environment. This requires a combination of optimism, realism, and self-empowerment. Self-empowerment in the construct of this book means "to give one's self the authority to be successful."

Although your environment, as well as others, will try to define what success should be for you as an individual, you are the only one who can truly define personal success. After all, no one can live your life for you but you. That is why there is a beginning and an ending to our individual mortality on this earth. In this light, time is a priceless commodity.

Personally, I have found that people waste an exorbitant amount of time on workplace behavior and communication that is nonproductive. As a person with a type A personality," I tend to have low tolerance for ineffectiveness and inefficiency. With this in mind, I found myself in a constant state of weariness and frustration for the first few years after undergraduate school. The outcome was my search for the ideal workplace utopia, changing jobs every two years. This was not a sustainable career strategy, especially for an independent, single female.

With wisdom and age, I learned that work ethic, prayer, and self-empowerment were the combined ingredients necessary (for me) for longevity in the workplace. My new perspective led me to focus on my True Authentic Self when in the wake of adversity. By developing my communication skills, I was able to stay at a job until I was ready to leave. More importantly, I made it a point to leave the organization/company with the same class and personal peace that I had when I first started.

It is not easy to develop the right combination of personal peace and success in your career. Sadly, adversity is sometimes more of a standard than an exception. For this reason, I hope that my testimony within this book will provide you with some intervention tools for becoming or staying positive and empowered in your professional career.

CHAPTER 4

Reconstructing Your Personal and Professional Career

I FIRST STARTED WORKING A professional-level job (while going to college) as an executive assistant to my mentor (Uncle Walter) in a nonprofit organization. The organization's mission was to facilitate economic development in an area that had been practically abandoned, in terms of capital city improvements, for over twenty years. If you can imagine a heavily blighted urban neighborhood in any city in America, that is what this two-mile corridor leading to downtown looked like. It was this experience that "fast tracked" my transition from my youthful naivety to the "real world" of business.

During this phase of my traditional workforce career (regular nine-to-five job), I had some incredible opportunities to meet a diverse group of politicians, entrepreneurs, nonprofit leaders, and public agency officials. On a traditional professional track, it probably would have taken me at least ten years to develop direct access to this same group of leaders.

It took my uncle twenty years of perseverance and patience to accomplish this urban transformation. In fact, he retired shortly after the transformation had come to fruition. Now when I visit my hometown, I marvel at the visual footprint of his work. Although my mother thought we were both a little "over the top" with community commitment, it was one of the best learning experiences I have ever had. The complexity of communication and adversity he confronted within his "life's work" has further reinforced my intrigue with human behavior and commitment to change.

My nonprofit experience served as the linchpin to all of my deliberate and unintentional professional experiences. I have captured some of them in this first book of the series titled *Imaginary Superstar*.

I will never forget something profound that Uncle Walter said to me when I was frustrated with a project we were working on. He said, "You are smart, but you have not lived life long enough." He was right; I was only twenty years old and a bit impatient with the lack of ethics, incompetence, and indifference I had observed.

I was especially disappointed in some of my observations within both the public and nonprofit sectors. I decided to validate whether my past experiences with the public sector were an exception, or the standard. As a result, I focused on getting hired in the public sector. I ended up working at every level of government within a ten-year period. As I had intended, this led to my ability to continue my advocacy for small businesses on a full-time basis and get paid for it.

After working at every level of government, including the US Small Business Administration (the best job I ever had), I decided to start my own management consulting practice. I felt that management consulting was the best method for me to assist executive leaders in transforming their organizations into productive and profitable enterprises. This consulting work was liberating, as I could be candid with my client-sponsors about their organizational challenges, personal accountability, and solutions for performance improvement.

Initially, the core competencies of my business were community relations, diversity training, executive coaching, and strategic planning. Occasionally, I would facilitate a planning meeting or fulfill a request for motivational speaking. Concurrently, I was teaching various undergraduate courses in business ethics, principles of management, strategic planning, and behavior and organizational conflict.

During the last several years, I immersed myself in my doctoral program in management, with a concentration on leadership and organizational change. After graduating, I now mentor both MBA and doctoral students as an adjunct professor of business.

My experience as both a scholar and practitioner has enabled me to develop a customized, holistic perspective for existing, new, or prospective leaders of the future. Each of these experiences enabled me to indulge my intrigue with human behavior and its interdependence with organizational culture.

I suppose that I have always been a social scientist, judging by my ability to identify both positive and negative patterns of human behavior/interaction in the workplace and its relationship to communication.

In today's rapidly changing business environment, strategic communication may not only neutralize negative behavior in the workplace, but it may also play a major role in facilitating sustainable leadership in the twenty-first century.

CHAPTER 5
The Stuff I Need to Do to Survive and Thrive

THIS BOOK SEGMENT PROVIDES STEPS for jumpstarting or resurrecting your professional status as a prospective, new, or existing leader who is willing to pierce the power of "the norm" to achieve facilitate positive, sustainable change. This will require an intense search of the inner self, looking inward and reflecting outward toward the "new self." The experiential exercises are designed to assist in comprehensive treatment of the entire cycle of self-transformation.

REFLECTION (PREWORK)

It seems that self-reflection is something that eludes many people. I believe this step is essential in today's leadership in complex organizations. In this book, the reader will enter into a dual connection between personal and professional reflection. This is important to note, as many people experience cognitive dissonance (self-conflict) in the workplace, simply because they have not found their "centeredness" as individuals. By centeredness, I mean the very essence of who you are, what is most important to you, and how well you manage the challenges that threaten your "authentic self-identity." When you do not know who you are, you can never attain sustainable transformation to who you want to become. If you are satisfied with who and where you are in your professional

18

life, then this principle does not apply to you. However, if you imagine yourself as an accomplished professional with many options for career transformation, then you may add the next section to your toolkit for success. Furthermore, if you imagine yourself as a superstar performer, your professional journey will be filled with lifelong learning as you develop principles for sustainable leadership.

EARNING THE RIGHT TO LEAD

Let's dig right into the foundation of leadership. I will first affirm that there is no universal theory for what leadership is or is not in the scholarly literature. However, I propose two controversial propositions of my own. First, in order to give direction, you must first learn to take direction. Second, you can be a leader, even though you have no followers. Each of these two propositions will be expounded upon in the subsequent section.

LEADERSHIP PROPOSITION #1

In order to give direction, you must first learn to take direction. You do not have a right to give directions until you have mastered the art of following direction. I have worked with or reported to many leaders in the past who did not give instructions with purpose, clarity, and productivity in mind. In some cases the consequences were negligible, but in others, they were catastrophic. Instead of becoming focused on the negative outcomes and complaints of fellow employees (relevant to leadership's direction), I tried to focus on a proactive reaction. If I felt strongly enough about the work related issue, I would present an alternative method to leadership for achieving the desired outcome. If my proposed methods were not acknowledged or unwelcomed, I chose to self-reflect on how I would have handled the situation (as a leader) differently, based on the information available to me. The point is there was still a learning opportunity for me based on my choice to learn from the leadership mistakes of others.

LEADERSHIP CHALLENGE #1:

Think of a time when you were given a directive or instructions on completing a task/project that was in conflict with what you felt was correct or ethical. Write a brief description of the situation and how the supervisor/leader communicated.

_____

_____

_____

_____

_____

_____

_____

_____

_____

_____

_____

_____

_____

_____

_____

_____

How do you believe the situation should have been handled?

_____

_____

_____

_____

_____

_____

LEADERSHIP PROPOSITION #2

You can be a leader, even though you have no followers. You can be a leader of one. However, you must first become the person that you would follow. For example, if you believe that a leader should be ethical, technically competent, and a great communicator, you must learn to master and exhibit those characteristics.

LEADERSHIP CHALLENGE #2:

Based on your past experience, as either a leader or a follower, what are the characteristics of a good leader?

a) _____

b) _____

c) _____

d) _____

e) _____

f) _____

g) _____

h) _____

i) _____

j) _____

LEADERSHIP CHALLENGE #3:

If you are or want to become a successful leader, which one of these characteristics listed in the Leadership Challenge #2 would you most need to improve? What are at least three steps you will take to improve in the next ninety days?

Characteristic	Description of Steps	Follow-up Date

SELF-REFLECTION EXERCISE #2:

Now that you have identified three specific steps that you will take over the next ninety days, I want you to honestly look inward: Would you follow someone with the knowledge, skills, and abilities that you currently possess?_____.

If yes or no, please state why. _____

_____.

Release

After reflecting on leadership characteristics, if you were able to honestly reflect on who you have been in the past and the characteristics that you must refine to move forward with your journey to being a superstar, then you are ready for the next step, to redirect.

Redirect

Becoming a superstar in the workplace requires accepting that you cannot achieve that status without others. This means that attaining superstar status is not just about you; it is about helping others become successful. This is not an easy concept to grasp in a society where individualism and instantaneous gratification is becoming the norm (instant messaging, Internet, social media, etc.). Although social media has created instant opportunities to connect, the effort required for developing individual and team accountability takes time. There is no shortcut to learning to communicate during the best and worst of times within the workplace. It is very easy to fall back into a state of indifference when you are impacted by a toxic workplace environment. However, redirecting positive (but genuine) behavior to deliberately overcome negativity may be the antidote for a toxic work environment.

SELF-REFLECTION EXERCISE #3:

What actionable item(s) will you practice relevant to positive communication in the workplace during the next seven days?

_____

_____

_____

_____

_____

Realign

Once you have done the work and identified your professional leadership areas of strength and weaknesses, it is important that you commit to specific changes that will enhance your ability to both lead and recruit others toward a productive and positive work environment. This is not an easy task, especially when your subordinates or team members may come from various cultures and age groups.

If you are new to an organization, it is easier to align yourself with your True Authentic Self (TAS), as there are usually no preconceived notions or expectations of your workforce behavior or communication. However, every organization has its own internal culture, in terms of acceptable behavior, communication, and business practices.

CHAPTER 6
Demographic Challenges of Leadership

CHANGES IN DEMOGRAPHICS, EDUCATIONAL, EDUCATIONAL levels, opportunities for women, and retirement age have created a mosaic of leadership opportunity. That means that leaders now have to become more rhetorically sensitive. By that, I mean that they will have to master the art of professional persuasion by adapting their communication skills to the varying demographics of the employees they manage. This is critical now more than ever. There are multiple generations of employees with varying ethnic, economic, religious, and educational backgrounds in many organizations. Younger employees are part of the technology, instant, and yes—

Sometimes overstimulated generation. However, they may also be more creative and open to new ideas. At the other end of the spectrum, you may have the experienced and more educated baby boomers exiting en masse to retire. As a result, some of the organizational memory may be lost.

The best part of the changing workforce demographics is that you may have a diverse group of employees from multiple generations. The challenging part is that you are the "linchpin" that holds the group together. I say linchpin, as opposed to glue, because a linchpin is the person who acts as the central figure for keeping the organizational/ business structure in place. When viewed with this lens, the organization is an active yet interdependent system that sets off a contagion of positive/negative behavior from the people within their sphere of influence. When leadership fails to sustain the connectivity of this interdependent system, organizational chaos follows.

The more a leader understands his or her critical role as a linchpin for stakeholder (employees, customers, board members, community, and etc.) "buy-in," the more adaptive the workforce will be when imminent organizational change and implementation are communicated throughout the organization.

THE TEMPLATE GENERATION

Along with the mixture of generations comes the complexity of what I call the "Template Generation." The Template Generation may be composed of any age group or individual, as it reflects a type of mind-set that results in characteristics of mental laziness. The outcome of this mind-set can become a primary saboteur of planned organizational change for leadership. The Template Generation represents one or more of the following characteristics:

- They want to know what the correct answer is, rather than moving through the process of discovery and research.
- They lack critical thinking skills (analysis, evaluation, etc.) and are offended when their thought process is questioned.
- They make decisions too quickly, without considering the relevant facts, due to their underlying need to look competent or take credit for others' work.
- They are lost when they have to transition from the abstract/unstructured to the concrete/structured. As a result, they complain to cover up for their incompetence or ignorance.

The business world is rapidly becoming complex, both in the domestic and global market. In this light, there is not always a single answer for solving complex business issues. Furthermore, the Template Generation mind-set may lead to catastrophic or irreversible damage to the organization.

As a professor of business many years ago, I told a group of students in my strategic planning course, "Because there are multiple ways to solve many business challenges, the answer is whatever you say it is, and you can defend it with a methodical process." This particular university used the "Socratic method" of teaching/learning, in which there were often long exchanges of question and dialogue. This gave the students an opportunity to reflect and think through their answers, based on guided dialogue and group interaction with both their student-peers and the instructor. This teaching method demonstrated the value of teamwork, peer-to-peer learning, critical thinking, and problem solving to my students.

The point I am making is that there is not always a clear answer to every question or challenge in the workplace. This emphasizes the critical role of the leader in figuring out the best solution through a series of inquiries and planned implementation of ideas. This leaves open the opportunity for creative problem solving and joint accountability.

CHAPTER 7

Planned Organizational Change and Contingency

LEADERS HAVE AN INCREDIBLE OPPORTUNITY for teambuilding and stakeholder buy-in when they are able to facilitate a transparent strategic planning process. During the planning process, there should always be time allotted for contingency planning. Any team or individual should take time to develop a contingency plan based on the data and current situation.

As a strategic planning facilitator, I have always been intrigued with the amount of tireless effort that organizations contribute to the formulation and implementation steps of the planning process. Yet they often abandon the evaluation and contingency planning process. Let me clarify this statement by saying that in these instances, the leadership team will document the entire strategic planning process, without actually evaluating the plan's progress or need for contingency plan implementation. This means that the team members are guaranteeing or hoping that their strategic plan will go exactly as documented, with no deviation or modifications needed. This is a grave mistake. Not only are real evaluation and contingency planning necessary components for attaining stakeholder engagement and accountability, but they are essential for planned organizational change.

It is necessary for leaders to communicate the outcome of the contingency planning and a method of progress updates. It is always a "red flag" for top leadership when employees/leaders are asking questions such as "Whatever happened to the strategic planning process that we spent a week working on?" This frustrates both those directly involved in the strategic planning process, as well as the organizational members. Most of all, it may ignite a lack of confidence in leadership, which may spark a firestorm of negativity throughout the planning group.

As a leader, it is your responsibility to make sure the strategic planning process is not only followed, but that it includes a contingency plan that will be reviewed at least every ninety days (if not sooner). Otherwise, the plan may become obsolete.

In today's complex business environment, large or small businesses may experience unanticipated consequences resulting from external forces (governmental, demographic, natural disaster, economy, etc.) that may not be within their control. However, unanticipated consequences caused by internal forces (R&D, financial operations, marketing, sales, technology, human resources, etc.) may often be avoided by analyzing past historical data for coming up with relevant modifications in advance. This is where contingency planning is most critical, as waiting more than ninety days to review/modify strategic business operations may be catastrophic.

A strategic plan should not be a static document. It should be like a finely tuned orchestra. It takes constant attention to every note for a well-composed and unified musical centerpiece. The leader must act as the maestro, able to adjust the chords and instrumentation of the symphony whenever necessary.

LACK OF COMMUNICATION CAN COST MILLIONS

I once had a client organization ask me to review a major contract relevant to a technology solution. The technology contractor for this project had been hired by one of the top decision makers of the company. The cost to date was several million dollars, yet the technology solution was not fully functional, as contracted. Sadly, the vendor had already been able to obtain approval for several contract modifications to resolve technical issues, of which they obviously did not have the technical competence to resolve.

My approach was to first review the contract for the documented scope of work, the deliverables, and the progress schedule. Then I reviewed the contract language for default and termination clauses. Based on my review, the vendor was in default, as the company had not been able to fully execute the technology solution as promised in the contract award. In addition, I found that the contract language allowed for a termination for default. Furthermore, this client was hemorrhaging financially and operationally, due to the vendor's incompetence.

My advice to the client was to terminate the contract (based on the termination clause for default). At this point, he could either directly advise the Senior Executive that it was a six-million-dollar mistake or terminate the contract. Or he could take the indirect route of giving him my report, which outlined the rationale for the contract termination. This was a critical decision-making opportunity, as this technology solution was key to the organization's strategic planning process. However, the strategic planning document had not been reviewed for evaluation or contingency planning. The company's direct consequence resulted in a multi-million dollar loss, as well as the cost of having to find another vendor to resolve this critical issue. Meanwhile, the vendor basically received a cash gift in excess of several million dollars (minus administrative costs), with no direct consequence.

The biggest challenge for my client (Ron) was how to communicate the recommendation to terminate to the Senior Executive (John) responsible for hiring the contractor. After all, John would be held responsible for not monitoring and reviewing the contract since its implementation. Ron's discomfort with a potential conflict between himself and the John seemed to be more of a concern to him rather than the consequence of lost millions. This was perplexing to me, as my client was also a senior executive r at the same organizational level. The lesson to be learned from this story is that "the mission of the organization is greater than any individual". Even though retaining professional relationships with your organizational peers is important, the implied trust between leadership and the organization's sustainability is of even greater importance.

CHAPTER 8

Workforce Warfare—The Stuff Nobody Told Me about Communication in the Workplace

AFTER PUTTING THIS BOOK DOWN for three months, I decided to review my writing for a fresh perspective. As I reflected, I noticed that many of the examples that I had written seem to have an underlying theme of managing bullying in the workplace. Although bullying is emerging as a very real challenge in school-age children, the impact is also very real within the workplace. Recently, I read an article in my local business journal focused on this very subject. The alternatives introduced included an internal policy on bullying and its potential consequences. My hope is that organizational leadership will begin to address this issue, as it may negatively impact employee recruiting, retention, and morale.

BULLYING TYPES IN THE WORKPLACE

For the purposes of this short book, I will provide several examples of how I have experienced bullying in the workplace by supervisors and coworkers. Even though I have always been a rather serious and empowered individual, I have still experienced the darkness and evil of workplace bullying.

DUAL RECIPROCITY EFFECT

It is not in my nature to provoke an altercation in my professional or personal life. However, I have never had a problem letting people know when they have crossed personal boundaries into areas of unacceptable behavior. Because I could be an impulsive person, during the early years of my career, I needed to develop professional communication skills that not only allowed me to maintain my calmness, but reflected the integrity of my ethics and professionalism. For me, this could only be done by developing what I call the "dual reciprocity effect."

I am defining the dual reciprocity effect as "taking a step back from the behavior of the other person, then responding in a way that not only communicates that the person's behavior is unacceptable but allows him or her the opportunity to respond in an acceptable fashion in the future". In other words, this communication strategy involves giving coworkers another chance (forgiveness) to be accountable, while allowing them an opportunity to receive the professional respect that was not given to me. For a reasonable, rational human being, this usually worked. For others, I had to use other measures (administratively) to move myself back to a place of personal peace. Rest assured, this dual reciprocity strategy worked for me, without losing my job, my mind, or my professional reputation.

The most powerful techniques I have discovered and used in the midst of workplace adversity are summarized with four general communication principles:

- Unless you are in physical danger, calm yourself for at least five to ten seconds. In some cases, you may just need to be quiet and ponder over the situation for twenty-four hours.
- Focus on the self-identified boundaries that empower (give yourself the authority) *you*, rather than the oppressor or the instigator/antagonist.
- Communicate those boundaries to the other person in an abbreviated fashion with canned lines that allow you to transition to

a peaceful demeanor. Canned lines might include phrases such as "I am struggling to understand..." or "I am confused by..." and take a breath, to give them an opportunity to respond or not. This technique is for your sake, rather than the other person's. In this light, if the other person responds negatively or positively, you have given him or her the opportunity to save face, clarify, or recover.

- Remember, retaining your professional integrity is the most important goal. Your response and reaction, not the other person's, is the primary source of positive energy. Empower yourself to act accordingly.

When there is a pattern of unacceptable behavior, you should address it as soon as you have calmed down. By pattern, I mean after the third time. This will prevent the other person from legitimately refuting your concerns by claiming that he or she does not know what you are talking about (either because they choose to forget, or too much time has passed). Be ready to provide the three examples of the undesirable behavior, just in case they claim that they do not know what you are talking about. One exception to this rule is in the case of sexual harassment and violence, which need to be addressed immediately with human resources or your immediate supervisor (assuming they are not the oppressor).

DEALING WITH SUPERVISORS' BULLYING BEHAVIOR

In this next segment, I have included several memorable experiences that exemplify how I was able to build my self-confidence in dealing with difficult people, whether my supervisor or a peer. Sadly, each of these types of examples demonstrates the bullying behavior that is not usually discussed in self-help books focused on strategies for getting hired, getting the right job, or dealing with difficult people.

In my first example, this particular supervisor was rather moody and expected me to modify my behavior based on how he was feeling on any given day. Unfortunately, he was the one who hired me, and we had to work closely together. He once impatiently came in my work area and stood in front of me while I was sitting down (with his private area within inches from my face). Not only was he in my personal space, but he was inappropriately creating the groundwork for a hostile environment.

Rather than being intimidated (or claiming sexual harassment), the first thing I did was compose myself calmly and project the professional demeanor that I expected from him. This enabled me to give him an opportunity to reflect on the inappropriateness of his behavior, and on the boundaries of my behavior "real-time."

My response: "Could you please back up within three feet? You are in my personal space in a way that is inappropriate." Thereafter, he respected that request and made sure that he did not stand closer than three feet when communicating with me during the tenure of my position there.

In my second example, this supervisor spent a great deal of time calling me into her office to gossip about people both inside and outside of the company.

My response: "I mean this respectfully, but I cannot listen to you talk about people, especially those for whom I have a great deal of respect; to listen to it is to become a part of it." She must have felt self-convicted from that day forward, as her vindictive behavior included antagonizing my direct-report staff and giving me a very low evaluation, although my team and I far exceeded the organization's performance goals in terms of revenues. This was probably the most challenging type of workplace bullying that I have experienced, as I was also a supervisor. This meant that the strife that I experienced with my division chief (supervisor) had to be completely transparent to my staff. Sadly, she made her personal conflict with the CEO known to me in the past. This further supported my belief that she had some personality challenges which had nothing to do with me. Eventually, I was able to transfer to another division, along with my staff. As a result, she was left with no supervisor or staff to supervise. Ultimately, she left the organization to accept an executive director position at a long-standing and well respected community non-profit. Within a year of her leadership (at the non-profit), there were allegations of "cooking the books", as well as other criminal allegations. The whole scandal "played out" in the local media over a long period of time. She was publicly disgraced.

If I had continued pacifying the negative behavior of my division chief (supervisor), I would have be out of alignment with my true authentic self (TAS). This would have caused me mental and physical stress. However, I was willing to accept the potential consequences in exchange for personal peace. In this light, there was no other alternative for me, personally. However, you as the reader, must decide if you are willing to accept the potential consequences that may come along with retaining your TAS and your personal peace, when in the midst of workplace adversity. In my example, the potential consequences never materialized. In fact, I learned two lessons. First, stay the course of positive behavior in alignment with my TAS and personal peace. Second, decide whether I am willing to accept the potential for negative consequences that may arise as a result of my communication approach.

Dealing with difficult supervisors can be a seemingly insurmountable challenge in and of itself. Some supervisors simply do not have the "soft skills" necessary to lead/manage others. In fact, they can barely lead or manage themselves, in some cases.

I have coached various professionals on how to deal with difficult supervisors. My advice was based on my own adversity, as well as the unfortunate difficulties of others. This book would be too voluminous to read if I tried to capture even a minuscule part of poor leadership variations I have observed. However, I am going to introduce the top five that I believe exemplify the phenomenon of poor leadership in the twenty-first-century workplace.

CHAPTER 9
Dealing with Peers' Bullying Behavior

AS A GRADUATE STUDENT, I learned many descriptive words for workplace behavior. However, one type of employee (in particular) remained in my business vocabulary over the years, due to its extreme negative impact on the organizational culture is a witchdoctor. A single employee exhibiting this behavior can actually derail "goodwill" in any organization, if this employee chooses to wield his or her position as a source of power.

One of the least-researched behaviors (in academia) observed in the workplace has been termed bullying (Trudel and Reio 2011). It is emerging as a legitimate organizational challenge that deserves remediation. While bullying is emerging as a legitimate workplace behavior that needs to be addressed, I do not believe that some of its covert and destructive ways have been fully articulated. This section will discuss several different types of nontraditional bullying that employees and leaders experience in today's contemporary workforce.

DISTINCTIVE COMPETENCIES RELEVANT TO BULLYING BEHAVIOR

Some organizations have employees who have distinctive competencies that enable a company to retain a competitive edge. However, internally, these employees can become artificially inflated with a "God Complex." In some circumstances, they can embody witchdoctor characteristics—that is, they are perceived as the only individuals who can perform these skills with the needed expertise. Without proper management, an organization can indirectly facilitate bullying behavior from employees in this critical skill category. This bullying can take the form of withholding information, unacceptable behavior and conduct, embarrassing or diminishing others, and other unacceptable types of behavior that are overlooked by those in positions of authority. Employees with these types of characteristics may wield critical expertise in order to maintain their sense of power and control.

Obviously, no company can afford to be held hostage by the bullying behavior previously discussed if it aspires to maintain or become a sustainable enterprise. In these instances, my question (directed to my coaching clients or leaders in general) is " What happens if that individual (with critical talent) dies, becomes ill, gets fired/transferred, or even loses their mind? "

I have personally experienced the effects of an employee who exhibited both the God Complex and witchdoctor characteristics many years ago. We were a small group of seasoned professionals, many of whom were a few short years away from retirement. Although we all used company computers to input data and provide services to our clients, several employees were uncomfortable with technical issues. As a result, they were heavily reliant on a single IT professional (witchdoctor) to resolve any technical issues. Sadly, this person would first verbally scold the employee into submission. Then she would fix the technical issue.

I was a confident, experienced, and seasoned professional with previous management experience. In this light, although I had heard of this coworker's abusive behavior, I thought that it would never happen to me. Finally, the day came when I requested her IT expertise for my computer. Unfortunately, she made the mistake of loudly scolding me and storming off to her work area. While this woman continued scolding me all the way across the entire building floor (to her desk), some nearby employees said, "Don't feel bad, she does that to everyone." I replied, "I don't care what she has done to everyone else. All I have to say is that she best fix my computer, or I will write her up." They gasped. I said, "That is an abuse of position. Therefore, if she does not fix my computer, knowing that she is the only one capable, I will write a formal complaint, even though I am not a supervisor."

Eventually, she returned to fix my computer a couple of hours later. However, that was not the end of her unprofessional tirade. She actually pointed her finger in my face and said, "Sit down." I did not move an inch. I softly replied, "Who are you talking to? If you make the mistake of hitting me while you are pointing at me, we are going to have problem." She then lowered her voice and masked her response by saying, "I was just asking you to sit down, so I can see the screen." When she finished the repairs, I gave her the respect that was not given to me by politely saying, "Thank you." To further extend my sincere professionalism, I made sure that I went by her office in the morning and said hello, as I normally did. After that, we never had a problem.

While I am certainly not saying that you, as the reader, should handle a bullying situation exactly the same way I did, I just want you to take a moment and think about how you would have handled this same scenario.

What would you have said or done if the same situation presented itself to you? Be honest. _____

_____

_____

_____

_____

_____

Is your response consistent with your TAS identified by you in the first section of this book? If not, what specific behaviors could you work on to build tolerance, while staying both professional and consistent with your TAS?

_____

_____

_____

The point I am trying to make is that everyone should be treated with dignity and respect, regardless of position or skill set. Although this particular situation with the IT expert may have been unique to this employer, this type of bullying behavior is not unusual. For those of you who aspire to greatness in alignment with your TAS, it is important that you consider this in responding to adversity in the workplace, especially when others are observing your responses. It may make a difference in your ability to get promoted, transferred, or even provide professional services (as I have) for that same company in the future.

In another example, I served as a temporary executive assistant at a particular organization after graduating from college and was horrified at some of the workplace behaviors that were tolerated there. There was a single employee who terrorized and bullied fellow employees. She would go into verbal tirades, cursing and making physical threats at whomever her victim of choice was for the day. On the other hand, she was extremely nice to me, bringing me trinkets and food. I was very suspicious and never ate anything she gave me. What was important to note was that the leadership team knew about her behavior and never addressed it. In fact, this behavior took place on several occasions in the presence of clients. After a few months, I left before my temporary assignment was completed. How could a leader allow this type of behavior "on his watch" with constituents observing?

REVERSE BULLYING AND COSMETIC SUPERVISING

Reverse bullying occurs when a leader is perceived to be a cosmetic supervisor. A cosmetic supervisor has the title, and perhaps the compensation, but no real power or influence over performance outcomes of his or her direct reports/employees. Here are some examples of this leadership type:

Type 1: They inherited staff from a supervisor who has left the organization.

I have experienced the challenges of inheriting a staff. Unfortunately, this group of fifteen people had developed some unacceptable behaviors and characteristics. Because they were physically in close proximity to each other (in a bullpen atmosphere, with no barriers), these behavior characteristics became both disruptive and counterproductive. Apparently, the previous supervisor had acted in the role of a "den mother," pacifying their tantrums and explosive verbal exchanges with each other "on the floor."

Because I had so many meetings, I was both unable and unwilling to closely monitor these seasoned professionals. Prior to actually supervising this group, I had a one-to-one, face-to-face session with each employee. During that orientation, I advised them what they could expect from me and vice versa. So, now was the time to demonstrate my sincerity in expectations of professional decorum. After hearing one loud, abusive verbal exchange, I advised that if they could not manage their differences professionally, I would intervene, without respect to the initiator of the disagreement and "write up" all parties involved with a performance warning (in compliance with the organization's code of conduct).

The previous scenario is important because leadership has the responsibility to develop a safe and productive environment for all employees. The hostile environment created by these employees may have escalated to workplace violence, employee turnover, and a loss of respect for my leadership, had I shirked my responsibilities. Furthermore, denying the serious nature of the unacceptable behavior was not going to alleviate its deafening presence. Thereafter, the employees operated in a professional manner under my leadership. Being a leader is not a popularity contest. When it comes to adversity in the workplace, the mission of the organization outweighs the mission of any individual. This business philosophy does not usually make you the most popular leader. However, being fair and equitable will more than likely lead to you being viewed as fair and consistent. This is a desirable outcome for those aspiring performance excellence and positive communication skills.

Type 2: They were assigned an employee without the benefit of participation in the hiring process.

I have two examples of colleagues who were not originally hired as supervisors yet assigned the responsibility for oversight and management of employees. Because they were not hired as supervisors, their direct reports ignored their authority to give direction and provide guidance.

In the first example, my colleague accepted the responsibility, without any preparation for the workplace culture. The outcome resulted in an employee telling her that she would never report to her. In other words, she was not going to accept guidance or feedback. Apparently, the employee had applied for the position but had been turned down. As a result, she exhibited passive-aggressive behavior toward my colleague that dictated corrective action.

In the second example (Type 2), my colleague (Selena) requested the hiring of an additional staff member to assist with the growing responsibilities. She formally requested to be a part of the hiring decision, as the skill set required was very niche-oriented. However, the hiring manager (Bob) ignored this request and hired someone (Jerry) who had not only demonstrated incompetence, but an unwillingness to learn. As a result, Jerry has compromised the successful contract performance in multimillion-dollar contracts. Furthermore, his unwillingness to learn has caused Selena productivity lost, due to the inordinate amount of time she has to spend correcting Jerry's mistakes. Although he was polite, Jerry was clearly in denial of his need for professional development. Furthermore, he tried to cloak his incompetence in the following ways:

- He moved quickly to take credit for solutions.
- He wanted to resolve problems too quickly.
- He didn't listen.

After Selena communicated Jerry's lack of performance to Bob (the hiring manager), he finally acknowledged the legitimacy of Selena's complaint. This was only due to his own personal experience in directly supervising Jerry while Selena was on an extended vacation. This is a sad commentary, as this scenario has been going on for three years. As a result, Jerry will be moved to another manager. In addition, they are supposed to be replacing his position with a new employee, as well as increasing Selena's salary for having to supervise them both (Jerry and the replacement hire) until the Jerry has been transferred. Sadly, this will not resolve the fundamental problem of an incompetent employee who refuses to learn or admit that he needs training.

Type 3: They were promoted to a position above their peers and are now afraid to supervise.

These are people who have been considered members of the "in crowd." Once they were promoted, it was difficult for them to accept the responsibility of communicating with their former colleagues in their new leadership roles. As a result, they are afraid of confrontation and exhibit avoidance behaviors with their former peers in the following ways:

- They overlook poor performance.
- They overcompensate to retain their friendships.
- They give preferential treatment.

Each of the three examples of reverse bullying provided in the previous section illustrates the need for emotional intelligence (Goleman 2006). There is no set method for managing communication in these scenarios. However, these kinds of situations do raise some interesting questions to be addressed or reflected upon by an aspiring or existing leader.

Effective leadership requires the ability to manage chaos, provide a safe zone for communication, and develop formal structures that enable both creativity and productive staff contribution. Each of these components dictates an adaptive yet reliable balance in the practice of leaders as teachers and learners of human development. No degree can provide these skills. However, observation, deliberate practice, and a willful intent can facilitate competence in these skills. The goal should be a continuous effort toward a sustainable organization through a human capital–focused approach. This approach is not effective if employees view leadership as disingenuous.

CHAPTER 10
Organizational Bullying

DURING MY EARLY TWENTIES, I worked for a corporation to pay my way through college. The job paid above minimum wage, had benefits, and offered flexible hours. Considering some of my previous jobs had been low paying and very physical, this was ideal; or so I thought. During my tenure at this job, I was a top performer many times over. My reward was company acknowledgement in the employee newsletter and celebrations, as well as the responsibility to train others. Initially, it seemed like an honor to train these individuals. However, the trainees were my peers, initially. After the training period, they were promoted, while I was never even given a courtesy interview. At first, I thought maybe it was because I was still a college student and that the trainees had already graduated. However, that was not the case. Then I noticed the lack of diversity in all levels of management.

Being the competitive person that I am, I found inequity in this scenario. When I inquired, no acceptable rationale was given. In fact, my evaluations supported my legitimate inquiry. With no reasonable rationale provided to me by human resources, I proceeded to document the unfair treatment, and then filed a complaint for racial discrimination. To make a long story short, the company's response to my discrimination charges resulted in the promotion of two employees of color to supervisory positions as a cover for discrimination. Of course I did not receive a promotion. However, I did have to endure supervisors regularly huddling together in a hallway to literally peer at me as I walked by. In addition, there were a litany of other behaviors which demonstrated a hostile work environment. Although I lost my case, I did leave when I found another position. I still provided the company with two weeks' notice, and was paid for my time in advance to leave. The point is, I left with "the same class and dignity" that I had coming into the organization.

Type 4: They have been promoted without earning the promotion.
Being a supervisor can make you a better person or a worse one. This is especially true for those who are promoted to leadership positions before they are ready. In this instance, they lack the soft or technical skills for the leadership promotion. If this is the case, it is the leaders' responsibility to acquire the necessary technical and communication skills, through learning and practice.

WHO CHECKS THE CHECKERS? (ETHICAL CONDUCT)
When those who hold positions of power violate trust, then comes the question of "Who checks the checkers?" If you are in a position of leadership, what policies and procedures are in place to ensure a balanced approach in business operations?

When those policies that affect the trust of organizational stakeholders (shareholders, board members, trustees, employee/members) have been violated, what consequences, if any, will be enacted?

You do not have to look very far in the media to see examples of leaders in positions of trust violating that trust through alleged corruption, theft, drug trafficking, sexual harassment, and more. The litany of malfeasance, misfeasance, and corruption is too long to recite.

We have leadership in every organization/business charged with the responsibility of being a model of social, professional, and ethical behavior. Unfortunately, the expectation of ethical behavior can sometimes bleed over into one's personal life as well. It is difficult to place leaders in the role of policy and decision makers when their public/personal behavior is contradictory. Although no one is perfect, it is important that leaders refrain from obvious impropriety. Impropriety, or even the perception of impropriety of leadership by employees, can quickly erode the morale and stakeholder buy-in, when it comes to positive cultural change.

VOLUNTEER BOARD LEADERSHIP AND ETHICAL BEHAVIOR

I have had the privilege of serving on various nonprofit boards in the past. Board leadership may provide you with an opportunity to utilize your professional skills to help bring about social change within your respective community. Idealistically, it may bring relief from the stress of your paid working career. However, this is not always the case. In some instances, you may experience a different type of stress in which you have absolutely no control, as will be discussed in this next segment.

Once upon a time, I experienced something very disheartening in my leadership experience. I was a board member of an organization that allowed the president to dictate matters of which the board had oversight and governance. In my observation, the board members blindly followed his self-perceived leadership. In fact, he had a fair amount of success and contribution to the community. However, his season was finished, whether he wanted to admit it or not. As my mentor used to say, sometimes you simply need to step down after one of your greatest victories and let the next generation have an opportunity.

I am sure that it was quite difficult for him to arrive at that conclusion. This manifested itself in characteristics of panicked behavior:
- suspected "cooking the books"
- attempts to pressure or intimidate board members
- refusal to provide necessary information for soliciting charitable donations
- intimidation of staff members

Before I was recruited as a board member, this organization apparently allowed the president to do whatever he wanted, based on his past successes. The trust exhibited between the board and the leader was completely imbalanced and unquestioned. Even in the midst of adversity and a critical need for cash infusion, the board acted as a cosmetic group of leadership, simply present to rubber-stamp his poor leadership and intimidating antics.

As a business professional and experienced nonprofit board leader and trainer, I could not continue my service in good conscience with the current state of things. Several of my colleagues shared my sentiments and agreed to a majority vote of "no confidence." Subsequently, we developed an approach that would enable the president to leave with dignity and transition to another position. However, the board president folded prior to the meeting and asked that we allow the president to appeal his eminent dismissal. Unfortunately, his appeal became an unacceptable tirade and confrontation between the board and the president. Sadly, he stayed in his position long after that episode and finally left. However, it was not soon enough, as he had already begun his campaign to intimidate both board members and staff.

Based on my experience and fiduciary responsibility, I decided that it was best that I simply resign and instead volunteer within a community organization that respected the checks and balances between the board and the organization's president.

CHAPTER 11
Toxic Work Environment

IN THE PREVIOUS CHAPTERS, YOU have learned a number of reasons why an organization can become toxic. However, it is important to acknowledge the tightly and loosely fitting interdependence of organizational structures. As complex as this proposition is, here is the key point: an organization can be dismantled and subsequently destroyed by a single individual within that structure, and that person does not have to have a position of power, merely of influence. Let me give you an example: At one former employer, I was a new department lead.

I reported to the department supervisor. When I was hired, it was based on the understanding that I would be trained by a counterpart (Mira) with the same position. However, her workload was to be divided between the two of us to provide her more relief. Rather than viewing this as an opportunity, she attempted to withhold information as a form of power.

In addition, Mira's style of caseload management was to intimidate others to make herself seem superior. Not only did she refuse to train me, but she would talk loudly about me to others, so I could hear.

Rather than get upset, as an empowered individual, I decided to read the regulations of the program and learn through trial and error. Using this approach, at minimum, would help me to become knowledgeable about the program policies and standard operating procedures, while not violating either.

Once Mira realized that I was not going to ask her again for assistance, she nicely asked if I was upset with her. My response (in alignment with my authentic self) was "Let's just do what we need to, relevant to being professional and performing our duties; otherwise, there is no need to be fake." While that may have seemed harsh, I simply did not want to take the time to be negative and give her power by rehashing her negative behavior. Thereafter, she and I had a very congenial and professional relationship.

In summary, this section discussed and provided examples of types of bullying in the workforce. It is my hope that you will use them as practice for how you would handle each of the scenarios in alignment with your TAS.

There is no single method for dealing with adversity, only our ability to self-reflect and communicate rationally, strategically, and with a willful intent for positive influence, when possible. In the next chapter, I have included seventeen tips, including a brief explanation, for surviving and thriving in workforce warfare.

CHAPTER 12

Survive and Thrive through Workforce Warfare

WORKFORCE SURVIVAL GUIDE: SEVENTEEN TIPS

I have included an abbreviated version of these seventeen tips in Appendix A. For your convenience, you can photocopy this short guide in case you need to refer back to it when you are working toward becoming a person of positive influence in the workplace.

Set a challenge to incorporate one or two of these tips each month for at least thirty days. Within a year, you will be on your way to becoming a person of positive influence (PPI) in alignment with your True Authentic Self (TAS).

1) **Demonstrate the importance of your professional image**
    Don't let anyone fool you about professional dress and etiquette. I graduated in the late 1980s. During this time period, we were taught the "old school" rules of business etiquette. I have listed some of them below:
    *   For interviews, wear a dark blue, gray, or black suit and blouse or a shirt and tie (for men).
    *   Wear dark shoes and socks or closed-toe shoes and pantyhose (for women).

- Wear conservative makeup and hairstyle, and not more than five pieces of jewelry, including your watch (for women)

The reason professional dress is important is twofold. First, you want the decision maker to be focused on the interview, rather than on distracting clothing, hair, or accessories. Second, it demonstrates the importance you place on the interview.

As I was once told, "It's easier to lighten up than to tighten up." This means that it will be easier to start off strict and then loosen up, as necessary. This same philosophy stands with professional dress. You should always opt for the traditional, professional dress, and if the workplace culture dictates otherwise, adjust accordingly. I don't mean dress casually because everyone else does. What I mean is that if the job is physical, or if you will be ostracized or not viewed as a team player, you will have to make the decision at that time. I can tell you that I always preferred to wear a suit, as it was easy to coordinate, and it feels good to me.

During the early stage of my business, I had several requests to present "Professional Business and Etiquette" workshops. This was due in part to the fact that the workplace was changing. The technology (dotcom) generation's influence had served as the catalyst for the seeming deterioration of human interaction and professional decorum. People had become too relaxed and were relying on the convenience of electronic communication as a surrogate for effective communication.

Here are some examples of business etiquette and professional dress violations:

- managers using e-mail to address performance issues, as a method of avoiding confrontation
- employees texting managers to notify them that they are taking sick time
- managers coming to work in spandex pants and short, waist-length blouses

- employees answering their mobile phones during work hours

These are just a few examples of how casual our work environment has become—too casual for professional communication and performance. Sadly, these examples include both leadership and management.

2) Be friendly but not familiar

This means that you greet people every day and where appropriate. However, you do not disclose personal details about your life and family outside a generic framework. For example, you might share that you are married with two children but not that you are married and separated or that your spouse is seeing a therapist. Following this communication strategy enables you to maintain the sociable yet professional decorum necessary for today's workplace, without providing fellow employees/supervisors the ability to leverage personal details for negative assumptions or sabotage.

3) Don't engage in gossip or "fire circles"

This means that you not only refrain from gossiping about others, but you do not listen to it either. This takes some communication strategy. In my personal experience, I had to give advance notification that I did not participate in gossip one person at a time. My coworkers would usually learn about refusal to engage in gossiping when they were gossiping about an employee or supervisor and I would suddenly announce that I had to leave and get back to my desk. If they happened to be in my office, I would ask them to leave (once they started gossiping) and say, "To listen to it is to be a part of it." It was not my intention to embarrass them but rather to illustrate the sincerity of my boundaries in "real time."

What I mean by "fire circles" is when a supervisor has a team meeting or group meeting and solicits feedback and participation from the group. Somehow, this may transform into a complaint session with no constructive feedback or alternative solutions for improvement. While I am not suggesting that a manager purposely encourages this nonproductive activity, on a repetitive basis it becomes an environment for negative communication.

In workplaces where fire circles are common, you may try two methods. First, try not to participate once you recognize this pattern. I pay attention but tend to doodle on a notepad in an effort to remain quiet.

Second, you may ask your supervisor if the group may be provided an agenda in advance of the meeting for the next time. If so, you can redirect the group by saying, "I am confused. Where is this item on the agenda?" As a last resort, you can summarize the complaints and ask if you understood them correctly, in an effort to either move the meeting in a positive direction or bring it to a conclusion.

4) **Limit your absenteeism to not more than three to five days (unless there is an unanticipated catastrophe or illness in your family)**
People sometimes confuse benefits with entitlements. Just because you are allotted five excused absences does not mean that you have to use them. With the exception of unanticipated illness of yourself or family members or catastrophic events, you should try to limit your benefit allowance to vacation or holidays. This will leave you with an image of organizational commitment (OC), irrespective of whether you feel that OC has been reciprocated to you. Furthermore, it contributes to a reputation for work ethic.

5) **Find out about company-sponsored professional development opportunities**
If your company sponsors professional development, such as tuition reimbursement, conferences, or work-related workshops, be sure to inquire and take advantage of the opportunities. If a company pays

for or reimburses professional development, it illustrates the value it places on employees' personal growth. In addition, when you take advantage of professional development opportunities, it shows that you have an interest in becoming a valuable player within the organization, as well.

6) Make sure that you do not contribute to employee negativity about the organization or leadership
As an IS, you may aspire to be a part of the leadership team. Some of the employee members you may engage with, relevant to the negativity, may aspire to be a part of leadership, as well. In this light, don't discount their potential insecurity about the negative things that you have witnessed them saying, or even what you yourself have said. Rather than trying to keep track of what "he said, they said, or you said," it is best to remove yourself from the situation. Eventually, other employees will note this pattern and either stop the negativity or gossiping, or they will anticipate and accept that you will not listen to or take part in the negativity activity.

In some instances, I was able to politely remove myself by making a suggestion or presenting a challenge. For example, on several occasions I heard complaints about compensation or inequities in pay. Often, this complaint would be accompanied with comparisons to other coworker's compensation. Because it is inappropriate to discuss salaries (in my opinion) with coworkers, I would say something like, "Can I make a suggestion?" If the person responded in the affirmative, I would state, "If you are unhappy with your salary and feel that you should be compensated more fairly, rather than compare yourself with someone else, speak on your own merit and state you case to the supervisor respectfully." This gave him or her an opportunity to bow out of the dialogue and do something about it or not mention it to me again.

7) Participate in company-sponsored volunteer activities

Company-sponsored volunteer activities not only offer an opportunity to take a break from the workplace but also to contribute to the organization within the internal and external community. Not only does it demonstrate your team member commitment, but it also shows that you are willing to go beyond expectations for the mission of the organization. Although it is not a guarantee, this may also be an informal method of interacting with leaders outside of your division.

Some leaders actually like to model the behavior they hope to elicit from their organizational members by actively participating in social/ informal events. In this instance, they (management) are outside of their formal role and willing to dialogue with members of every level of the organization. Make sure you take this opportunity to personally introduce yourself. If nothing else, managers/executive leadership will remember your face if they see you at multiple volunteer activities. Eventually, they may recognize your name, too.

8) Share bright ideas or suggestions when solicited and unsolicited by the company

If you have ideas or solutions for improving some aspect of organizational performance, try to find a formal or informal avenue for sharing those ideas. For example, one company that I worked for had a "bright idea" box for employee suggestions. If your idea was adopted, you received formal recognition.

If your organization does not have a formal avenue for sharing ideas, perhaps you may suggest an anonymous suggestion box or recognition event, as I have shared above. Alternatively, your reputation for volunteerism may gain you entrée to an informal environment in which you have access to leadership to share your ideas.

9) Develop canned lines to manage adversity in the workplace

As previously discussed, you need to develop your own individual communication style for managing adversity, irrespective of your role in the workplace. The purpose of adopting this practice is to maintain your individual integrity and professional behavior. In other words, the precanned lines are for your sake, not the oppressor's.

10) Be early or on time for work and work-related activities

Work ethic includes the habit of timeliness, whether showing up for work, scheduled meetings, or other work-related activities. Being late should always be an exception. People notice when someone is always timely (with little exception). They also take note when someone is chronically late. Although habitual tardiness might be addressed as a joke and an accepted behavior, it is a symptom of a lack of work ethic.

I can't think of anything more disrespectful of others than being chronically late for a meeting. This is totally unacceptable for a leader (especially when he or she is leading/facilitating the meeting). It is disrespectful for those who have planned and were on time. Moreover, I think it is unfortunate that these same individuals expect someone to stop or interrupt the meeting and catch them up.

11) Don't violate your personal values/ethics

The problem with violating your core personal values/ethics in collusion with, or even under pressure from, a peer or supervisor is that there is an underlying expectation that you will repeat that same behavior. In this light, once you reach an internal state of conflict with your TAS, you will have to make a grand choice. The decision you make now (at this point), may determine the number of options you will have later. Most importantly, it will determine how you and others will view you for your entire employee life cycle at the company.

12) **Develop your writing skills**

Having command of the written word still has power and influence. This may be true whether you are an employee or leader. If there are opportunities within your organization to contribute to the company newsletter, blog, or other social media, it may assist you in showcasing your talents in multiple ways.

13) **Develop your presentation skills**

Developing refined oratory skills may make the difference between attaining a promotional opportunity or not. Try volunteering to conduct verbal presentations as a team leader/employee in various situations (departmental meetings, training, briefings, etc.), especially when a volunteer is needed. This may be an opportunity to demonstrate your ability to facilitate, persuade, or motivate others to success.

14) **Stay a part of relevant professional associations**

It is easy to stay within your comfort zone of predictability, especially if you are in a stressful or toxic work environment. In these circumstances, it is so challenging to get through the day, all you want to do is go home and not think about anything work related until the next week begins. This may be a grave mistake, as you need a positive environment outside of work where you can control your ability to develop and network with others within your discipline.

Volunteering within professional associations may lead to opportunities to not only develop your leadership skills but to network with decision makers at other companies. In addition, it will give you professional development opportunities and a sense of accomplishment.

I had a colleague (John) who was the president of a professional association while in the midst of a very stressful career. During his tenure as president of the association, he was contacted about potential candidates within his group for a six-figure income opportunity with an international firm. He notified the group of the job opportunity, but no one was interested. Subsequently, he was asked if he would be interested. He applied and is still working there almost ten years later. Not only has it been a substantial increase in pay for him, but an opportunity to increase his national exposure and professional reputation in his field.

15) Stay mentally alert

Irrespective of your position or the culture of an organization, continue to stay mentally alert. There is nothing worse than managing or being managed by an individual who is mentally lazy. What I mean is that the person deliberately refuses to learn within his or her position. Mentally lazy people do the bare minimum and are reluctant to increase their knowledge and creativity in their position.

As a supervisor, I encouraged my employees to seek opportunities to learn by researching first, then asking for help later. When an employee tries to find the answer him- or herself, it increases their knowledge, as well as their self-confidence in their abilities. In addition, it reduces the number of times the supervisor has to clarify or explain a process, simply because an employee has not taken the time to learn the concept at all.

16) Continuously work on developing your critical thinking skills

Critical thinking skills are invaluable for an employee in becoming a direct contributor to any organization. By developing critical thinking skills, an employee may problem solve by first, considering the known facts, and then establishing relevant connections in a way that transitions from the abstract to the concrete, thereby developing potential solutions for organizational success.

The flowchart below illustrates the critical thinking process.

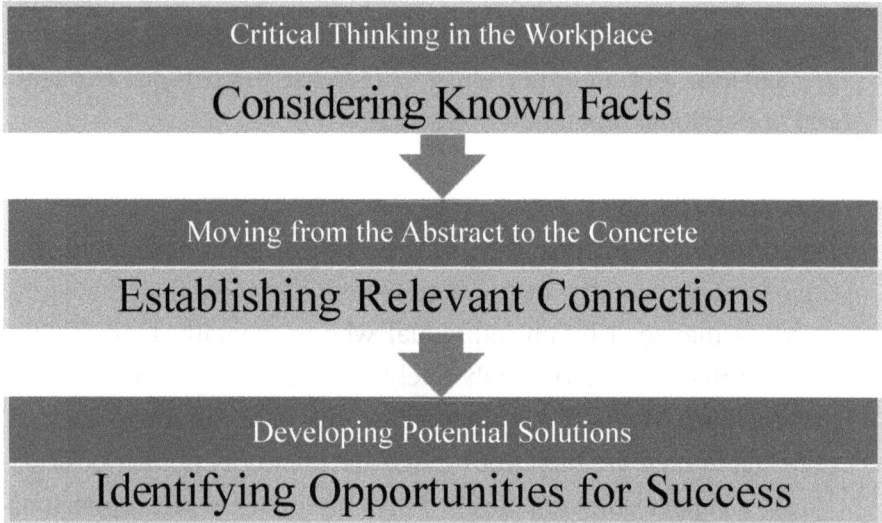

CRITICAL THINKING PROCESS

Critical Thinking in the Workplace

Considering Known Facts

Moving from the Abstract to the Concrete

Establishing Relevant Connections

Developing Potential Solutions

Identifying Opportunities for Success

The secret to superior critical thinking skills (in my opinion) is to deliberately cultivate a great memory and a yearning for reading. This entails purposefully memorizing both direct and indirect facts about a variety of subjects: politics, business, sports, education, and life. Learning about each of these areas increases both the breadth and depth of your personal and professional knowledge. A great bonus to this approach is that it keeps a continuous capacity for new knowledge and creative solutions. In today's competitive workplace, organizations are continuously seeking employees with new and creative ideas for sustainability.

17) Stay physically alert and healthy
Looking and feeling physically alert may improve your outlook at work, even in the midst of a stressful or toxic workplace. Anytime you have to deal with uncertainty in communicating with varying

personalities, it is important that you feel your physical best. Even as a self-employed management consultant and part-time professor, I still start my day off with at least an hour of exercise (cardio and weights) to ensure that I start off with a good day. Even if you exercise at the end of your day, it will assist in staving off the potential effects of stress and negativity within the workplace. At minimum, you will feel a sense of control and accomplishment every day.

Workplace warfare can erode an individual's personal self-worth, professional value, and work ethic at any organization or company where people do not reciprocate mutual respect for human dignity. In the end, you, as an individual, have to decide what your TAS looks like before fully challenging a work environment that does not have an internal moral and social conscience.

In some instances, good people feel trapped by the financial obligations which cause them to stay with an organization that invokes irreparable damage and stress. Keeping this in mind, the best prevention is to create professional options, including "living within your means."

If you are two paychecks from being homeless (I am exaggerating), then there are limited options for exiting an organization that is causing you an immeasurable amount of stress, anxiety, and constant drama. What may appear as a financial decision of endurance may become a mental journey to a living death. In some cases, it may become a physical journey to an early death. Only you can decide how to manage the effect of work related stress.

Alternatively, you may choose to commit to your quest for superstar performance and personal peace, without compromising your integrity. The outcome may sound unattainable. But take baby steps and just commit to transforming your perspective on how you view adversity in the midst of workforce warfare. Maybe you will emerge with the superstar potential that you always imagined.

Hopefully, you will add the seventeen tips I have provided to your professional toolkit for surviving and thriving through workforce warfare.

After thirty years of working in various roles (manager, employee, consultant, and entrepreneur), I have finally figured out that becoming an Imaginary Superstar *realized*, is an evolving journey toward professional excellence and personal peace. To that end, I will continue to share my journey and lessons learned with others, in the hope that they will garner some ideas and personal inspiration in their own quests toward performance excellence and personal peace.

Conclusion

THIS BOOK REFLECTS AN ABBREVIATED testimony to my professional career over the last thirty years. Today's workplace is not only complex from an organizational standpoint, but it is complex from a human capital (people and talent) standpoint.

If you are just starting your professional career after college, reentering the workforce, or starting a new position or career, I hope that this book has been a source of reflection as you begin the next chapter of your life. Everyone can be a source of positive self-empowerment, influence, and superstar potential. Don't give up—just keep looking up toward your full human potential!

Stay tuned for the next installment of the *Imaginary Superstar* series
Installment 2 (Volume 2)
To be announced in December 2014 on our website!
Subscribe to our mailing list at **www.imaginarysuperstar.com**

References

Goleman, D. *Social Intelligence: The Revolutionary New Science of Human Relationships.* New York: Bantam Books, 2006.

Trudel, J., and Reio, T. G. "Managing Workplace Incivility: The Role of Conflict Management Styles—Antecedent or Antidote? *Human Resource Development Quarterly 22* (2011), 395–423. doi:10.1002/hrdq.20081.

Appendix A: Workforce Warfare Survival Desktop Checklist

1) Demonstrate the importance of your professional image.
2) Be friendly but not familiar.
3) Don't engage in gossip or "fire circles."
4) Limit your absenteeism to not more than three to five days (unless there is an unanticipated catastrophe or illness in your family).
5) Find out about company-sponsored professional development opportunities.
6) Make sure that you do not contribute to employee negativity about the organization or leadership.
7) Participate in company-sponsored volunteer activities.
8) Share bright ideas or suggestions when solicited and unsolicited by the company.
9) Develop canned lines to manage adversity in the workplace (for your sake).
10) Be early or on time for work and other work-related activities.
11) Don't violate your personal values/ethics.
12) Develop your writing skills.
13) Develop your presentation skills.
14) Stay a part of relevant professional associations.

15) Stay mentally alert.
16) Continuously work on developing your critical thinking skills.
17) Stay physically alert and healthy.

About the Author

DR. WANDA CORNER IS A scholar practitioner. She is currently an adjunct business professor, mentoring MBA and doctoral students In addition, she has continued her scholarly research in the areas of leadership and entrepreneurship, working collaboratively with other scholars.

Dr. Corner has also been a self-employed management consultant for the last fourteen years for a diversified portfolio of clients in every business sector. This has included but not been limited to public, nonprofit, corporate, and small business enterprises. At this juncture in her professional career, she primarily focuses her business on executive coaching and organizational change. Her approach to leadership integrates the performance accountability of entrepreneurship into every coaching, strategic planning, and consulting project. As a motivational speaker, her signature topics include: a) Sustainable Leadership in the Twenty-First Century, b) Self-Empowerment, and c) The Entrepreneur's Truth. She now lives with her husband in Atlanta, Georgia. She enjoys reading, writing, exercising, and relaxing with family and friends.

www.ingramcontent.com/pod-product-compliance
Lightning Source LLC
Chambersburg PA
CBHW060641210326
41520CB00010B/1698